TELL ME
ABOUT
EXPLORERS

THOR
HEYERDAHL

written by
John Malam

Evans Brothers Limited

Published by Evans Brothers Limited
2A Portman Mansions
Chiltern Street
London W1M 1LE

© Evans Brothers Limited 1997

First published 1997

Printed by Graficas Reunidas SA, Spain

British Library Cataloguing in Publication data.

Malam, John
  Thor Heyerdahl. - (Tell me about explorers)
  1.Heyerdahl - Thor, 1914- - Juvenile literature 2.Explorers
  - Norway - Biography - Juvenile literature
  I.Title
  910.9'2

ISBN 0237517639

Thor Heyerdahl is a famous explorer from Norway. He has always wanted to find out about people from long ago. He thinks they might have sailed across the world's oceans in search of new land. To see if his ideas could be true, he has gone on some exciting journeys. This is his story.

Thor Heyerdahl

Thor Heyerdahl was born in 1914, in Larvik, a small fishing town in the south of Norway.

When he was a boy, Thor liked to explore the world around him. He walked along the coast, and into the countryside. He collected sea shells, butterflies and animals such as lemmings and hedgehogs. Once he even brought a poisonous snake home!

Thor learned to ski when he was very young.

Thor's house in Larvik, in Norway

When Thor was fourteen, he went on holiday with his mother to the mountains. Each day they went walking across the moors.

On one of their walks they met a man called Ola Bjorneby. Ola said that he lived all alone on the wild moors. He said that he used to live in a town, just like Thor. Ola lived a simple life. There was something about it that Thor liked.

Thor liked walking on the wild moors of Norway.

At home in Larvik, Thor wondered if he could live a simple life too, just like Ola. It would mean living far away from modern towns, in a place where he would feel close to nature.

Thor read about the tiny islands in the Pacific Ocean. They were on the other side of the world. He wondered what it would be like to live there.

Thor dreamed of living on a small Pacific island like this one.

When he was old enough, Thor went to Oslo University to learn about animals. When he was there his teacher said that he should go to an island and study the animals there. He must find out how the animals crossed over the sea to get to the island.

At university, Thor met Liv Torp. She wanted to live on an island too. Thor and Liv were married on Christmas Eve, 1936. On Christmas Day they set off on their island adventure.

Oslo, capital of Norway, where Thor was a student

Thor and Liv sailed to Fatu Hiva. It was a beautiful island in the Pacific Ocean. It was so far away it took more than nine weeks to get there.

Fatu Hiva was very different to Norway. There were no cars or trains, and no electricity.

There was plenty of fresh food on the island. They picked bananas, oranges, mangoes, tomatoes and coconuts. They caught prawns in a river.

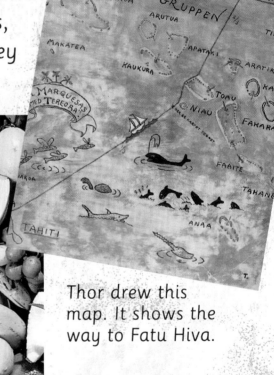

Thor drew this map. It shows the way to Fatu Hiva.

All these exotic fruits grow on Pacific islands

Thor's friend Tioti

Thor made friends with people on the island. Tioti showed Thor an old carving of a strange boat. Tei-Tetua told Thor an old story about how the first people came to Fatu Hiva. He said a god called Kon-Tiki had brought them across the sea from a land far away. Tei-Tetua pointed in the direction of South America.

Thor and Liv's home on Fatu Hiva

Thor and Liv stayed on Fatu Hiva for one whole year. Then they went home to Norway.

The story about the god Kon-Tiki, and the strange boat carving, had given Thor an amazing idea. In those days, experts thought the first people to live on the islands of the Pacific Ocean had sailed there from Asia. But Thor said they had sailed from South America. He set out to show he was right.

Thor at home in Norway

Thor knew that long ago the people who lived in South America had made balsa wood rafts. He went to South America and built a big raft from balsa wood and bamboo. He called it "Kon-Tiki", after the god in the old story.

On the 27 April, 1947, the "Kon-Tiki" sailed from Peru, in South America. On board were Thor and five of his friends.

Thor used bamboo (left) and balsa wood to build the "Kon-Tiki" (below). Many people said the raft would sink.

The "Kon-Tiki" bobbed up and down like a cork. It did not sink. The wind and sea current carried the raft far across the Pacific Ocean.

After 100 days, the "Kon-Tiki" landed on a Pacific island. Thor had shown that long ago people from South America could have sailed to the Pacific islands.

Thor became famous. But there were still people who did not believe his idea.

Thor caught a shark and pulled it on to the "Kon-Tiki".

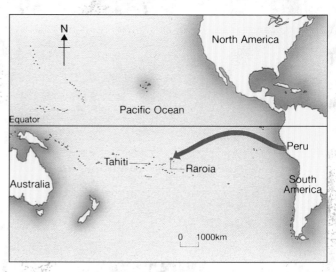

Thor sailed the "Kon-Tiki" across 6,400 kilometres of dangerous seas

Thor looks at a huge statue on Easter Island.

A few years after his "Kon-Tiki" adventure Thor went to an island in the Pacific Ocean called Easter Island.

Thor looked at the island's mysterious stone statues. He saw that some statues had long ears and earrings. He knew that the people of South America wore earrings just the same.

Thor hoped this discovery would make people change their minds and believe in his idea.

Thor's next adventure was when he sailed across the Atlantic Ocean. He wanted to find out the answer to this question: "Could people from long ago have sailed from Africa to America?"

Thor made a boat out of reeds. The reeds came from the papyrus plant. He used reeds because this is what the ancient people of Egypt and South America had used. If people from Africa had gone to America, then perhaps they had sailed in reed boats.

People in South America still make boats out of reeds.

The reed boat "Ra II" in which Thor crossed the Atlantic Ocean

Thor called his boat "Ra", after the ancient Egyptian sun god. His first boat was damaged in a storm. Thor built another one and called it "Ra II". He set out from Morocco, in Africa. After fifty-seven days at sea he reached the West Indies, a group of islands near the coast of America.

Once again, Thor had shown that people from the past could have sailed across the world's seas.

17

Thor's last sea adventure was in a reed boat called "Tigris". He sailed across the Indian Ocean, along a route once used by traders, and landed in the small country of Djibouti, in Africa.

Building the "Tigris"

During the voyage, Thor had seen how dirty the seas were becoming. In Africa there were wars and many homeless people. It made him feel sad and angry. He decided to do something to show how much he cared about our planet.

Thor set fire to the "Tigris" in Djibouti harbour.

His reed boat was soon a mass of orange flames, sinking into the water.

In a letter to the leaders of the world, Thor said that people should help one another, or else our beautiful planet would be turned into a sinking ship, just like the "Tigris".

The "Tigris" goes down in flames.

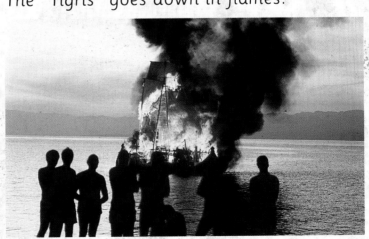

Thor Heyerdahl has spent his life exploring the mysteries of the world. He believes the people of the past were explorers too, crossing the seas to find new land. His adventures have tried to show how clever those people really were.

The boats that Thor Heyerdahl used on his adventures are as famous as he is. Today, "Kon-Tiki" and "Ra II" are kept in a special museum in Oslo, in Norway.

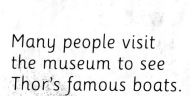

Many people visit the museum to see Thor's famous boats.

Important dates

1914	Thor Heyerdahl was born in Norway
1937-1938	He lived for a year on Fatu Hiva, an island in the Pacific Ocean
1947	He sailed the "Kon-Tiki" across the Pacific Ocean
1955	He led an expedition to Easter Island
1969	"Ra I" sank in the Atlantic Ocean
1970	He sailed "Ra II" across the Atlantic Ocean
1977-1978	He sailed the "Tigris" across the Indian Ocean
1982-1984	He worked on the Maldives, a group of islands in the Indian Ocean
1986-1988	He worked again on Easter Island

Thor wearing an ancient crown, on Fatu Hiva

Keywords

Atlantic Ocean
the second largest ocean in the world

balsa wood
a light wood that floats well

Indian Ocean
the third largest ocean in the world

Pacific Ocean
the largest ocean in the world

papyrus
a tall water plant

raft
a group of floating logs tied together with ropes

Index